VERY EASY TRUE STORIES

A PICTURE-BASED FIRST READER

by Sandra Heyer

Longman

To my parents, Ed and Irma. How lucky I am to have you; how wonderful it is for all of us to gather for "the usual" and tell our true stories.

Very Easy True Stories:
A Picture-Based First Reader

© 1998 by Addison Wesley Longman, Inc.
All rights reserved.
No part of this publication may be reproduced,
stored in a retrieval system, or transmitted
in any form or by any means, electronic, mechanical,
photocopying, recording, or otherwise,
without the prior permission of the publisher.

Pearson Education, 10 Bank Street, White Plains, NY 10606

Editorial director: Allen Ascher
Acquisitions editor: Louisa Hellegers
Director of design and production: Rhea Banker
Managing editor: Linda Moser
Production manager: Marie McNamara
Associate production editor: Robert Ruvo
Manufacturing supervisor: Edie Pullman
Cover design: Curt Belshe
Text design: Curt Belshe
Text composition: ElectraGraphics
Text art: Don Martinetti
Photo credits: see page 90

Library of Congress Cataloging-in-Publication Data

Heyer, Sandra
    Very easy true stories : a picture-based first reader / by
    Sandra Heyer.
        p.   cm.
    ISBN 0-201-34313-4
    1. English language—Textbooks for foreign speakers.   2. Readers
for new literates.   I. Title.
PE1128.H4363   1998
428.6'4—dc21

                                                97-49657
                                                    CIP

7 8 9 10—CRS—03 02

Contents

Introduction

Very Easy True Stories is a first reader for students of English as a Second Language (ESL). It is for absolute beginners who are familiar with the Roman alphabet, as well as for students with well-developed speaking and listening skills but low-level literacy skills. The stories are written in the present tense, in the simplest and most concrete language possible.

Very Easy True Stories contains fourteen units, each centered on a story that was adapted from a newspaper or magazine article. In answer to those students who think that some stories are too amazing to be true: *Yes, the stories are true.* The penguin really does do his own shopping, and the man really did find $2,000 in his fast-food bag. All of the stories were verified by reputable news sources.

Each unit is divided into three sections: Pre-Reading, Reading, and Post-Reading Exercises. Following are some suggestions for using each of the sections. Teachers new to the field might find these suggestions especially helpful. Please keep in mind that these are only suggestions. Teachers should, of course, feel free to adapt these strategies to best suit their teaching styles and their students' learning styles.

PRE-READING

The pre-reading drawing introduces the theme of the story. It also facilitates teaching of essential vocabulary and prompts students to recall knowledge and experiences that will help them understand the story. Here is one possible sequence of steps for using the pre-reading drawing.

1. With the help of the pre-reading drawing, elicit the vocabulary of the story.

Ask students to turn to the pre-reading drawing in their books. (Or make a transparency of the pre-reading page, and show it on the overhead projector.) Ask students, "What do you see?" Write their responses on the board, on flash cards, or directly on the transparency. (Some teachers advocate printing in block letters, rather than in upper- and lowercase letters, since block printing is easier for students to copy.) As you write, say the words slowly to model correct pronunciation. Students copy the words onto the picture in their books.

If all the students are absolute beginners, it is unlikely they will be able to supply the vocabulary for the pre-reading drawing. Instead of asking students, "What do you see?" begin by simply labeling the items and actions depicted in the drawing and slowly pronouncing the words. Say only five or six words. That's plenty for beginners. Resist the inclination to talk to yourself as you label ("Let's see . . . and over here there's a . . .").

2. Tell students what the story is about.

Point to the title of the story and read it aloud slowly. Then connect the vocabulary of the pre-reading drawing to the title. For example, say, "This story is about a penguin," as you point to the penguin in the drawing. Say, "The penguin goes shopping," and point to the word "shopping" in the title. As students progress through the book, try to stop at "This story is about . . . ," and see if students can use the pre-reading drawing and the title of the story to make predictions about the story.

READING

Following is one possible sequence of steps in reading the story:

1. Read the story aloud to the students.

Ask students to turn to the second and third pages of the unit, which are in comic-strip format. Tell students to look at just the drawings for now, not at the words beneath the drawings. The purpose of this first reading is to give students a global, not a word-for-word, understanding of the story.

Read the story aloud as students look at the drawings. Begin by saying, "Number one," and slowly read the sentence that the first drawing illustrates. Then say, "Number two," and read the appropriate sentence. Continue in this manner. Saying the numbers of the pictures while telling the story ensures that all eyes are on the same picture.

If your students are absolute beginners, you might need to break the story down into even smaller chunks of meaning when you tell it. In Unit 1, for example, the second sentence is, "He lives with a family in Japan." Instead of reading the sentence exactly as it is written, you might point to the man in the drawing and say, "Father" (or "Papa," if that is a cognate for your students), point to the woman and say, "Mother" (or "Mama"), and point to the child and say, "Child." Circle the trio with your finger and say, "Family." Digress again to explain "Japan" by pointing to Japan on a world map or by drawing a sketch on the board. Then go back to picture 2 and say, "He" (pointing to Rara) "lives with a family" (pointing to the family) "in Japan" (pointing to Japan on a world map).

You will probably want to walk away from the pictures from time to time and act out some scenes, perhaps with the help of props. (The teacher who field-tested "Shopping Day" came to class with a backpack, fish cut out of paper, and a shopping basket borrowed from a local supermarket.)

Some of the stories build suspense. You might stop short of the last few sentences when reading those stories aloud and let students—silently—read how the story ends.

2. Read the story a second time.

This time, however, instruct students to look at the words beneath the pictures.

3. Give students time to read the story silently.

Some students will be ready to go to the fourth page and read the story in text form. Other students will need to read the story in comic-strip format so that they can go back and forth between the words and the pictures to check their understanding.

4. Present the story in a different way.

If students have a global understanding of the story but need practice mastering its language, you might try one of these activities:

• Read the story aloud, but this time, make "mistakes." ("Rara is a dog. He lives with a family in New York. Every Tuesday Rara goes shopping.") Pause after each sentence, letting students speak in chorus to correct the mistake, rather than calling on individuals. A variation of this technique is to make mistakes in only *some* of the sentences. Students say "Yes" if the sentence is correct, "No" if it isn't. (Some teachers like to give each student two differently colored index cards. On one card "YES" is printed; on the other card "NO" is printed. After hearing each sentence, students hold up the card with their answer.)

• Read the story aloud, sentence by sentence, and ask the entire class to repeat, echoing your pronunciation, intonation, and rhythm.

• Read sentences from the story at random. Students call out the number of each corresponding picture.

• Say key words in the story. Students scan to find the words and circle them; they can verify their work by checking with a partner.

Teaching Young Students

If you teach young students, you may need to use one of the four activities above instead of, not in addi-

tion to, having students read the story on their own. Adults understand that looking at the pictures while hearing the story is a helpful pre-reading step; children see it as an end unto itself. Middle school students who participated in field-testing *Very Easy True Stories* were somewhat puzzled by the teacher's request that they read the story silently. They had just heard the story, and they knew how it ended. Why would they want to read it? When, however, reading the story was made into a game, they were enthusiastic readers. They especially liked identifying mistakes in the teacher's version of the story and scanning for key words (an activity which they turned into a race to see who could find the words first).

Teaching Absolute Beginners

Very Easy True Stories was field-tested in several ESL environments. One of those environments was a class of zero-level adult learners, all native speakers of Spanish. Before beginning Unit 1, the teacher told his students—in Spanish—that they were going to hear and read a story. He told his students not to worry about understanding every word, but to try to get the gist of the story. He said that in the course of reading the story, maybe they'd learn a couple of new words, and that would be great! Those few words in Spanish instantly changed the atmosphere in the classroom: The students went from looking apprehensive to looking relaxed in a matter of seconds. Their goal had changed from the impossible to the possible—instead of trying to understand every word, they were just going to enjoy the story and maybe pick up a few new words (a goal they did, in fact, accomplish).

If you have absolute beginners in your class, it is well worth the effort to find people—more advanced students in the same class, perhaps, or in another class in your program—to make a similar announcement in your students' native languages. When you do find native speakers to make the announcement, consider asking them to write it for you so you'll be able to encourage future students in their native languages.

THE POST-READING EXERCISES
Pronunciation

In some units, the exercise section begins with a pronunciation exercise. This exercise groups words in the story according to their accented vowel sound. Students, especially those whose first language is phonetic, are usually surprised to discover that the five English vowels make more than five sounds. In the course of the book, the pronunciation exercises acquaint students with thirteen vowel sounds. The purpose of the exercises is simply to make students aware that these sounds exist in English, not to drill students into pronouncing the sounds perfectly. (In fact, doing so would probably be a disservice. Keep in mind that some vowels make one sound when they are stressed, as they are in the exercise, but change to the neutral vowel /ə/ when they are in an unstressed position. Consider how the pronunciation of the "a" in "and" changes when "and" is put in an unstressed position: "cream and sugar.")

Spelling

This exercise is a dictation exercise. For absolute beginners, write the words on the board so that they can copy them. More advanced students like to work this exercise like a puzzle, trying to figure out the word from the letters given and announcing it before the teacher can say it.

Vocabulary, Comprehension, and Writing

Students can complete these exercises individually, in pairs, in small groups, or with the whole class. The exercises can be completed in class or assigned as homework. At the back of the book there is an answer key to the exercises.

Discussion

These exercises personalize the themes of the stories. They are written at a level parallel to that of the readings; that is, they assume that students speak and write about as well as they read. As a result, these exercises introduce no new vocabulary; the vocabulary consists solely of words recycled from the story. If, however, your students are fairly proficient speakers, you will probably want to encourage them to talk about the stories, asking them, for example, if they, like Mrs. Zimmer, have ever been stranded, or if, like Erik, they have ever gotten lost in a big city.

You could let the discussion lead into a writing activity, using the Language Experience Approach. Briefly, the Language Experience Approach consists of these steps:

1. The student orally relates a story or experience.
2. The teacher writes the student's words (sitting next to the student so the student can see what is being written).

3. The teacher reads the story.
4. The student reads the story.

These steps can be done as a group activity, which is ideal for multilevel classes. In order for students as a group to be able to dictate sentences, though, you will have to first create a group experience, such as a field trip, or draw on a situation the students have in common. For example, students in a class of young adults separated into two groups after reading the story "Neighbors." The men were given a blank piece of paper with the heading "The Perfect Wife" and the women were given a blank piece of paper with the heading "The Perfect Husband." The men collaborated to make a list of the attributes of a perfect wife, dictating their sentences to a teacher's aide ("She is a good cook." "She has long hair."), while the women dictated their sentences to the teacher. The two groups then came together to read one another's lists.

Keep in mind that the first step in the Language Experience Approach is an oral one. If your students are zero-level speakers of English, you will not want to venture from the controlled speaking exercises in the book.

Students in a beginning ESL class can have a wide range of experience with English, as you may know only too well. Some students are at zero-level in all the skills areas: reading, writing, speaking, and listening. Other students may have well-developed speaking and listening skills, but low-level literacy skills. Another group may have studied English in their native countries, perhaps for years, and are fairly proficient readers and writers, but were placed in a beginning class because they are unable to speak or understand spoken English. So, you may have to tamper with the exercises—to adjust them up or down, to skip some, or to add some of your own. Both the exercises and reading selections are intended to build students' confidence along with their reading skills. Above all, it is hoped that reading *Very Easy True Stories* will be a pleasure, for both you and your students.

Very Easy True Stories is the first book in the *True Stories* reading series. It is followed by *Easy True Stories, True Stories in the News, More True Stories,* and *Even More True Stories.*

UNIT **1**

Shopping Day

1. PRE-READING

- Look at the picture. What do you see?
- Say the words.
- Watch your teacher write the words.
- Copy the words onto the picture.

2. READING

- Listen to your teacher read the story. Look at the pictures.
- Listen to your teacher read the story again. Look at the words. Read the story.

1

Rara is a penguin.

2

He lives with a family in Japan.

3

Every Monday Rara goes shopping.

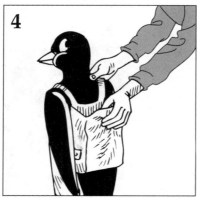

4

Rara's family puts a backpack on Rara's back.

5

Rara walks to the fish market.

6

He looks at the fish at the market.

7

He takes 12 small fish.

8

He eats the 12 fish.

9

Rara takes some fish for his family.

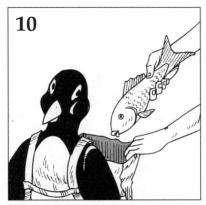

10

A woman puts the fish in Rara's backpack.

11

Rara walks home with the fish.

12

Rara's family takes their fish out of his backpack.

13

"Good penguin!"
Rara's family says.
"Thank you, Rara!"

• **Read the story again.**

Shopping Day

Rara is a penguin. He lives with a family in Japan.

Every Monday Rara goes shopping. Rara's family puts a backpack on Rara's back. Rara walks to the fish market. He looks at the fish at the market. He takes 12 small fish. He eats the 12 fish.

Rara takes some fish for his family. A woman puts the fish in Rara's backpack. Rara walks home with the fish.

Rara's family takes their fish out of his backpack. "Good penguin!" Rara's family says. "Thank you, Rara!"

3. PRONUNCIATION

Listen to your teacher. Say the words.

is	**a**	p**u**t
h**is**	**o**f	l**oo**k
f**is**h	s**o**me	g**oo**d
w**i**th	M**o**nday	w**o**man
in		

4. SPELLING

Listen to your teacher say the words. Write the missing letters. Then copy the words.

1. f _a_ mil _y_   _family_

2. M___nd___y   _____

3. ba___k   _____

4. wa___k   _____

5. lo___k   _____

6. tak___   _____

7. h___me   _____

8. t___a___k   _____

5. VOCABULARY

What do you see in the pictures? Write the words.

penguin
backpack

12 small fish
fish market

every Monday
a family in Japan

1. _fish market_   2. _____   3. _____

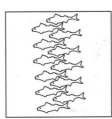

4. _____   5. _____   6. _____

6. COMPREHENSION

Which sentence is correct? Circle a or b.

1. **a.** Rara lives with a family in Japan.
   b. Rara lives at a market in Japan.

2. **a.** Every day Rara goes shopping.
   b. Every Monday Rara goes shopping.

3. **a.** Rara looks at the fish at the market.
   b. Rara looks at the backpacks at the market.

4. **a.** Rara eats two small fish.
   b. Rara eats twelve small fish.

5. **a.** Rara takes some fish for a woman.
   b. Rara takes some fish for his family.

6. **a.** "Thank you!" Rara's family says.
   b. "How are you?" Rara's family says.

7. WRITING

Write the sentences correctly.

1. Raraisapenguin.

   Rara is a penguin.

2. EveryMondayRaragoesshopping.

   _____

3. Hewalkstothefishmarket.

   _____

4. Heeats12fishatthemarket.

   _____

5. Hetakessomefishforhisfamily.

   _____

6. Hewalkshomewiththefish.

   _____

Mary Walks Home

1. PRE-READING

- Look at the picture. What do you see?
- Say the words.
- Watch your teacher write the words.
- Copy the words onto the picture.

2. READING

- Listen to your teacher read the story. Look at the pictures.
- Listen to your teacher read the story again. Look at the words. Read the story.

1

Mary works at a bank.

2

She begins working
at eight o'clock
in the morning.

3

She stops working
at five o'clock
in the afternoon.

4

At five o'clock
the bank closes.

5

Everybody goes home.

6

Some people drive home.

7

Some people take
the train.

8

Some people take
the bus.

9

Mary walks home.

10 She likes to walk.

11 She walks, and walks, and walks, and walks.

12 Mary lives eight miles[1] from the bank.

13 She walks for three hours.

14 At eight o'clock in the evening, Mary is home.

15 She eats dinner.

16 At ten o'clock she goes to bed.

17 Mary is tired. She is 82 years old.

---

[1] 12.9 kilometers

• Read the story again.

Mary Walks Home

Mary works at a bank. She begins working at eight o'clock in the morning. She stops working at five o'clock in the afternoon.

At five o'clock the bank closes. Everybody goes home. Some people drive home. Some people take the train. Some people take the bus.

Mary walks home. She likes to walk. She walks, and walks, and walks, and walks. Mary lives eight miles[1] from the bank. She walks for three hours.

At eight o'clock in the evening, Mary is home. She eats dinner. At ten o'clock she goes to bed. Mary is tired.

She is 82 years old.

---

[1] 12.9 kilometers

3. VOCABULARY

What do you see in the pictures? Write the words.

drive   take the bus   eat dinner
take the train   walk   go to bed

1. _go to bed_

2. _____

3. _____

4. _____

5. _____

6. _____

4. COMPREHENSION

Which sentence is correct? Circle a or b.

1. **a.** Mary lives at a bank.
   (b.) Mary works at a bank.

2. **a.** She begins working at eight o'clock in the evening.
   b. She begins working at eight o'clock in the morning.

3. **a.** At five o'clock the bus closes.
   b. At five o'clock the bank closes.

4. **a.** Mary walks home.
   b. Mary drives home.

5. **a.** She walks for three hours.
   b. She walks for eight hours.

6. **a.** Mary doesn't like to walk.
   b. Mary likes to walk.

5. WRITING

Complete the sentences.

1. Mary works from eight to five.

   Mary _works_ from _eight_ to five.

   Mary _____ _____ _____ to _____.

   _____ _____ _____ _____ _____ _____.

2. Then she walks home.

   Then she walks _____.

   _____ she walks _____.

   _____ _____ _____ _____.

3. She walks for three hours.

   She _____ for _____ hours.

   She _____ for _____ _____.

   _____ _____ _____ _____ _____.

4. Mary likes to walk.

   Mary likes _____ walk.

   _____ likes _____ walk.

   _____ _____ _____ _____.

6. DISCUSSION

Mary walks three hours every day. And you? Check (✓) your answer.

_____ I walk three hours every day.   _____ I walk 30 minutes every day.

_____ I walk two hours every day.   _____ I walk 15 minutes every day.

_____ I walk one hour every day.   _____ I don't walk every day.

Now count your classmates. How many people walk three hours a day? How many people walk two hours a day? One hour a day? Thirty minutes a day? Fifteen minutes a day? How many people don't walk every day? Who is the champion walker in your class?

Elevator Romance

1. PRE-READING

- Look at the picture. What do you see?
- Say the words.
- Watch your teacher write the words.
- Copy the words onto the picture.

2. READING

- Listen to your teacher read the story. Look at the pictures.
- Listen to your teacher read the story again. Look at the words. Read the story.

A young man gets on an elevator.

The elevator goes up.

The elevator stops. A young woman gets on the elevator.

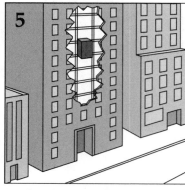

The elevator goes up. Then it stops.

It doesn't go up. It doesn't go down. It is stuck between floors.

The elevator is stuck for 19 hours.

The man and the woman are in the elevator. They are together for 19 hours.

They talk, and talk, and talk.

Finally, the elevator goes up.

10

It stops, and the doors open.

11

The man and the woman walk out of the elevator.

12

They are tired.

13

They are hungry.

14

They are thirsty.

15

They are in love.

16

Three months later, they get married.

• Read the story again.

Elevator Romance

A young man gets on an elevator. The elevator goes up. The elevator stops. A young woman gets on the elevator. The elevator goes up. Then it stops.

It doesn't go up. It doesn't go down. It is stuck between floors.

The elevator is stuck for 19 hours. The man and the woman are in the elevator. They are together for 19 hours. They talk, and talk, and talk.

Finally, the elevator goes up. It stops, and the doors open. The man and the woman walk out of the elevator.

They are tired. They are hungry. They are thirsty. They are in love. Three months later, they get married.

3. SPELLING

Listen to your teacher say the words. Write the missing letters. Then copy the words.

1. ta_l_k   _____talk_____

2. w___lk   _____

3. t___r___d   _____

4. ___un___ry   _____

5. t___irs___y   _____

6. mo___t___   _____

7. ___ate___   _____

8. m___rr___ed   _____

4. VOCABULARY

What do you see in the pictures? Write the words.

a hungry woman   two people in love   an elevator
a thirsty man   a tired woman

 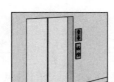  

1. _a hungry woman_   2. _____   3. _____

4. _____   5. _____

5. COMPREHENSION

Which sentence is correct? Circle a or b.

1. **a.** Three young men are in an elevator.
   (b.) A young man and a young woman are in an elevator.

2. **a.** The elevator is stuck on the fourth floor.
   b. The elevator is stuck between floors.

3. **a.** The elevator is stuck for one hour.
   b. The elevator is stuck for nineteen hours.

4. **a.** The man and the woman talk and talk.
   b. The man and the woman walk and walk.

5. **a.** Three months later, the man and the woman get hungry.
   b. Three months later, the man and the woman get married.

6. WRITING

Complete the sentences.

A young man and a young _____woman_____ are in an elevator. The
                                    1
elevator is _____ between floors.
                       2
The man and the woman are in the _____ for 19 hours.
                                            3
They talk and talk.

Finally, the elevator goes up. It stops, and the doors_____.
                                                                  4
The man and the woman are tired, hungry, and _____. They
                                                        5
are also in _____ .
                    6

7. DISCUSSION

Answer the questions. Raise your hands. Count the people.
How many people are . . .

1. hungry? _____   4. married? _____

2. thirsty? _____   5. in love? _____

3. tired? _____

A Son for Mr. and Mrs. Aversa?

1. PRE-READING

- Look at the picture. What do you see?
- Say the words.
- Watch your teacher write the words.
- Copy the words onto the picture.

2. READING

- Listen to your teacher read the story. Look at the pictures.
- Listen to your teacher read the story again. Look at the words. Read the story.

1

Mr. and Mrs. Aversa have two daughters.

2

They love their daughters very much.

3

But they want a son, too.

4

Mrs. Aversa is expecting a baby. "Maybe it's a boy," Mr. and Mrs. Aversa think.

5

Mrs. Aversa goes to the doctor. The doctor says, "There are four babies!"

6

"Four babies!"
Mrs. Aversa says.
"Maybe one baby is a boy."

7

Mrs. Aversa goes to the hospital.

8

The first baby is born.
"It's a girl!" the doctor says.

9

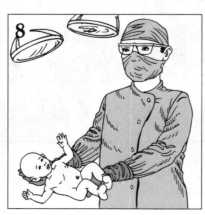

The second baby is born.
"It's a girl!" the doctor says.

10

The third baby is born.
"It's a girl!" the doctor says.

11

The fourth baby is born.
"Another girl!"
the doctor says.

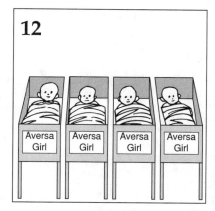

12

All four babies are girls.

13

Now Mr. and Mrs. Aversa
have six daughters.

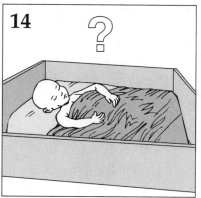

14

Do they want more
babies—maybe a son?

15

"No," Mr. and Mrs. Aversa
say. "We're happy with
six daughters."

• Read the story again.

A Son for Mr. and Mrs. Aversa?

Mr. and Mrs. Aversa have two daughters. They love their daughters very much. But they want a son, too.

Mrs. Aversa is expecting a baby. "Maybe it's a boy," Mr. and Mrs. Aversa think. Mrs. Aversa goes to the doctor. The doctor says, "There are four babies!"

"Four babies!" Mrs. Aversa says. "Maybe one baby is a boy."

Mrs. Aversa goes to the hospital. The first baby is born. "It's a girl!" the doctor says. The second baby is born. "It's a girl!" the doctor says. The third baby is born. "It's a girl!" the doctor says. The fourth baby is born. "Another girl!" the doctor says. All four babies are girls.

Now Mr. and Mrs. Aversa have six daughters. Do they want more babies—maybe a son? "No," Mr. and Mrs. Aversa say. "We're happy with six daughters."

3. PRONUNCIATION

Listen to your teacher. Say the words.

love son another but much	doctor hospital want	to too two do	their there very	more four born

4. SPELLING

Listen to your teacher say the words. Write the missing letters. Then copy the words.

1. l _o_ ve   _____love_____

2. ver___   _____

3. mu___h   _____

4. do___t___r   _____

5. b___b___es   _____

6. ___n___the___   _____

7. da___g___te___   _____

8. s___n   _____

5. VOCABULARY

What do you see in the pictures? Write the words.

the first baby   the fourth baby   the second baby   the third baby

1. <u>the first baby</u>   2. _____

3. _____   4. _____

6. COMPREHENSION

Complete the sentences. Write the letter of your answer.

1. Mrs. Aversa is expecting __c__

2. Mr. and Mrs. Aversa want _____

3. The doctor says, _____

4. All four babies are _____

5. Now Mr. and Mrs. Aversa have _____

a. girls.

b. "There are four babies!"

c. a baby.

d. six daughters.

e. a son.

7. WRITING

Complete the sentences.

Mrs. Aversa is _____expecting_____ a baby. She and her husband want a
                        1
boy because they have _____ daughters.
                              2
The _____ says, "There are _____
        3   4
babies!" Mrs. Aversa thinks, "Maybe one baby is a boy."

Mrs. Aversa goes to the hospital. The first baby is born. It is a

_____. The second _____ is born. It is a
        5   6
girl. The third baby is born. It is another girl. The _____
                                                              7
baby is a girl, too.

Now the Aversas have six daughters. Do they want _____
                                                              8
babies—maybe a son? "No," the Aversas say. "We're happy with six daughters."

8. DISCUSSION

How many children are there in your family? How many boys? How many girls?
Complete the sentences.

In my family, there are _____ children.

There are _____ boys.

There are _____ girls.

Read your sentences to the class.

Is There a Face on Mars?

1. PRE-READING

- Look at the picture. What do you see?
- Say the words.
- Watch your teacher write the words.
- Copy the words onto the picture.

2. READING

- Listen to your teacher read the story. Look at the pictures.
- Listen to your teacher read the story again. Look at the words. Read the story.

1

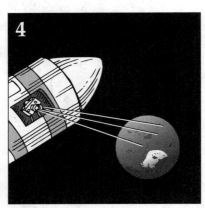

It is 1976.

2

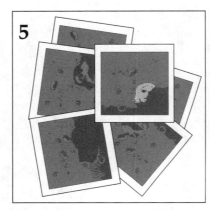

A spaceship goes up.

3

It goes to Mars.

4

There is a camera
in the spaceship.

5

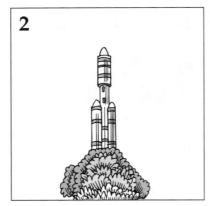

The camera takes photos
of Mars.

6

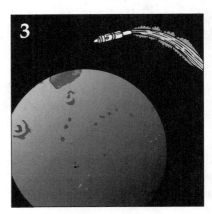

In one photo, there is
a face on Mars.

7

The face has eyes, a nose,
and a mouth.

8

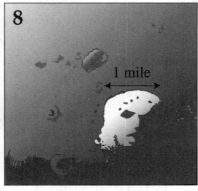

The face is big—
it is one mile[1] wide.

9

The photo is
in many newspapers.

---

[1] 1.6 kilometers

10

People look at the photo.
"Look!" the people say.
"There's a face on Mars!"

11

"No," scientists say.
"It's not a face."

12

"It's a hill."

13

"Light and shadow make
the face. Look. Here's
the light."

14

"Here's the shadow."

15

What do you think?

16

Is it a face? Or is it light
and shadow on a hill?

Is There a Face on Mars?

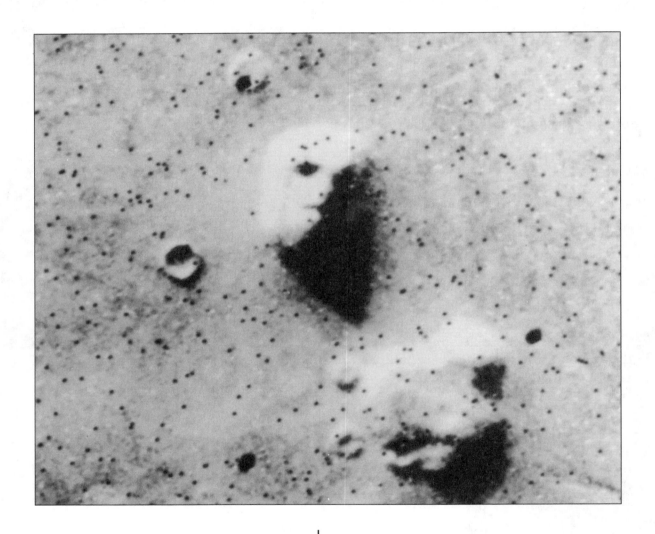

It is 1976. A spaceship goes up. It goes to Mars.

There is a camera in the spaceship. The camera takes photos of Mars. In one photo, there is a face on Mars. The face has eyes, a nose, and a mouth. The face is big—it is one mile[1] wide.

The photo is in many newspapers. People look at the photo. "Look!" the people say. "There's a face on Mars!"

"No," scientists say. "It's not a face. It's a hill. Light and shadow make the face. Look. Here's the light. Here's the shadow."

What do you think? Is it a face? Or is it light and shadow on a hill?

---

[1] 1.6 kilometers

3. PRONUNCIATION

Listen to your teacher. Say the words.

up **of** **a** what	**at** **has** **and** shadow camera	take face say make space	go photo no nose

4. SPELLING

Listen to your teacher say the words. Write the missing letters. Then copy the words.

1. ta_k_ e   _take_

2. fa___ e   _____

3. ne___s___ap___r   _____

4. pe___p___e   _____

5. ___ide   _____

6. hi___l   _____

7. l___g___t   _____

8. t___in___   _____

5. VOCABULARY

What do you see in the pictures? Write the words.

spaceship   face   shadow
newspaper   hill   scientist

1. _hill_   2. _____   3. _____

4. _____   5. _____   6. _____

6. COMPREHENSION

Complete the sentences. Write the letter of your answer.

1. A spaceship __c__

2. A camera in the spaceship _____

3. In one photo, _____

4. The face _____

5. Scientists _____

a. there is a face.

b. say, "Light and shadow make the face."

c. goes to Mars.

d. has eyes, a nose, and a mouth.

e. takes photos.

7. WRITING

Complete the sentences. Write your answer on the line.

1. Where does the spaceship go?

   It goes to _____ **Mars** _____ .

2. What is in the spaceship?

   A _____ is in the spaceship.

3. What does the camera do?

   It _____ photos of Mars.

4. What is in one photo?

   There is a _____ in one photo.

5. How big is the face?

   It is one _____ wide.

6. What do scientists say about the face?

   They say, "It's not a face. It's light and _____ on a hill."

Neighbors

1. PRE-READING

- Look at the picture. What do you see?
- Say the words.
- Watch your teacher write the words.
- Copy the words onto the picture.

2. READING

- Listen to your teacher read the story. Look at the pictures.
- Listen to your teacher read the story again. Look at the words. Read the story.

1

Jack and Ann are married.
They are not happy
together. Why not?

2

They are very different.
Jack smokes.
Ann doesn't smoke.

3

Jack likes to watch
baseball on TV.

4

Ann doesn't like baseball.

5

Ann likes loud music.

6

Jack doesn't like
loud music.

7

Jack snores at night.
Ann can't sleep.

8

One day, Ann looks
at the house next door.
It is for sale.

9

Ann buys the house
and moves in.

10

Now Ann lives
in the house next to Jack.

11

In his house, Jack can
watch baseball on TV.

12

He can smoke.

13

He can snore.

14

In her house, Ann can
listen to loud music.

15

She can sleep.

16

Now Jack and Ann are
married *and* happy!

• **Read the story again.**

Neighbors

Jack and Ann are married. They are not happy together. Why not?

They are very different. Jack smokes. Ann doesn't smoke. Jack likes to watch baseball on TV. Ann doesn't like baseball. Ann likes loud music. Jack doesn't like loud music. Jack snores at night. Ann can't sleep.

One day, Ann looks at the house next door. It is for sale. Ann buys the house and moves in.

Now Ann lives in the house next to Jack. In his house, Jack can watch baseball on TV. He can smoke. He can snore. In her house, Ann can listen to loud music. She can sleep.

Now Jack and Ann are married <u>and</u> happy!

3. PRONUNCIATION

Listen to your teacher. Say the words.

like night buy why	it is lives different	Ann Jack can can't happy	baseball they day	loud house now	for snore door

4. VOCABULARY

What do you see in the pictures? Write the words.

move in   snore   watch baseball on TV
smoke   listen to music

1. _smoke_

2. _____

3. _____

4. _____

5. _____

5. COMPREHENSION

Complete the sentences. Write the letter of your answer.

1. Jack and Ann are not happy _b_

2. Jack smokes, _____

3. Jack likes to watch baseball on TV, _____

4. Ann likes loud music, _____

5. Jack snores, _____

a. but Jack doesn't like loud music.

b. because they are very different.

c. and Ann can't sleep.

d. but Ann doesn't like baseball.

e. but Ann doesn't smoke.

6. WRITING

Write the sentences correctly.

1. JackandAnnaremarried,buttheyarenothappy.

   Jack and Ann are married, but they are not happy.

2. Theyareverydifferent.

   _____

3. Annbuysthehousenextdoor.

   _____

4. Shemovesin.

   _____

5. NowAnnisJack'sneighbor.

   _____

7. DISCUSSION

Circle YES or NO.

1. I am married.   YES   NO
2. I am happy today.   YES   NO
3. I smoke.   YES   NO
4. I like to listen to loud music.   YES   NO
5. I like to watch baseball on TV.   YES   NO
6. I snore.   YES   NO
7. I think Jack and Ann have a good idea.   YES   NO

Read your sentences and your answers to a partner.

A Smart Mother

1. PRE-READING

- Look at the picture. What do you see?
- Say the words.
- Watch your teacher write the words.
- Copy the words onto the picture.

2. READING

- Listen to your teacher read the story. Look at the pictures.
- Listen to your teacher read the story again. Look at the words. Read the story.

1

This is Tasha.
She has six puppies.

2

Tasha lives with Gary.

3

Gary lives in California.

4

It is raining in California.
It is raining hard.

5

Water is in the streets.

6

Water is in the houses.

7

Water is coming
into Gary's house.

8

He runs to his car
with his clothes.

9

He runs to his car
with his books.

10

He runs to his car
with his TV.

11

Oh, no!
Tasha and her puppies!
They are in the yard.

12

Gary runs to the yard.

13

The water is two feet[1]
deep.

14

Where is Tasha?

15

There she is!
She is swimming.

16

Where are the puppies?

17

There they are!
They are in a plastic bowl.
It is Tasha's food bowl.

18

Tasha is pushing the bowl
with her nose.
The puppies have
a smart mother.

[1] .6 meter

• **Read the story again.**

A Smart Mother

This is Tasha. She has six puppies. Tasha lives with Gary. Gary lives in California.

It is raining in California. It is raining hard. Water is in the streets. Water is in the houses.

Water is coming into Gary's house. He runs to his car with his clothes. He runs to his car with his books. He runs to his car with his TV.

Oh, no! Tasha and her puppies! They are in the yard!

Gary runs to the yard. The water is two feet[1] deep. Where is Tasha? There she is! She is swimming. Where are the puppies? There they are! They are in a plastic bowl. It is Tasha's food bowl. Tasha is pushing the bowl with her nose.

The puppies have a smart mother.

---
[1] .6 meter

3. VOCABULARY

What do you see in the pictures? Write the words.

puppies   clothes   yard
California   books   bowl

1. <u>California</u>

2. _____

3. _____

4. _____

5. _____

6. _____

4. COMPREHENSION

Circle YES or NO.

1. It is raining hard.	(YES)	NO
2. Water is in the streets and in the houses.	YES	NO
3. Water is in Gary's car.	YES	NO
4. Gary runs to his car with his clothes, books, and TV.	YES	NO
5. Tasha is Gary's dog.	YES	NO
6. Tasha has two puppies.	YES	NO
7. Gary runs to his car with Tasha and her puppies.	YES	NO
8. Tasha and her puppies are in the yard.	YES	NO
9. The water is two feet deep in the yard.	YES	NO
10. Tasha's puppies are in a plastic bowl.	YES	NO
11. Tasha is pushing the bowl with her nose.	YES	NO

5. DISCUSSION

Tasha is Gary's pet. Which pets do you see in the pictures? Your teacher will write the words. Copy the words under the pictures.

1. _____

2. _____

3. _____

4. _____

Ask a partner the questions. Circle your partner's answers.

1. Do you want a hamster?   YES   NO
2. Do you want a cat?   YES   NO
3. Do you want a rabbit?   YES   NO
4. Do you want a bird?   YES   NO
5. Do you want a dog?   YES   NO
6. Do you want a fish?   YES   NO

Stuck!

1. PRE-READING

- Look at the picture. What do you see?
- Say the words.
- Watch your teacher write the words.
- Copy the words onto the picture.

2. READING

- Listen to your teacher read the story. Look at the pictures.
- Listen to your teacher read the story again. Look at the words. Read the story.

1

Three men are in a truck.
The men are Sam, Joe,
and Tom.

2

The truck is pulling
a house.

3

The men drive under
a bridge.

4

The truck stops. Why?
The house is stuck. It is
stuck under the bridge.

5

The men get out
of the truck.

6

They look at the house.
They have a problem!

7

Joe says, "Maybe we can
pull the house out!"

8

Sam says, "Maybe we can
push the house out."

9

Tom looks under
the house.
He looks at the tires.

He lets some air out
of one tire.

The men let air out
of all the tires.

Now there is half an inch[1]
between the house and
the bridge. The house is
not stuck!

The men get
into their truck.

They drive away
with the house.

---

[1] 1.26 centimeters

Stuck!

Three men are in a truck. The men are Sam, Joe, and Tom. The truck is pulling a house.

The men drive under a bridge. The truck stops. Why? The house is stuck. It is stuck under the bridge.

The men get out of the truck. They look at the house. They have a problem! Joe says, "Maybe we can pull the house out."

Sam says, "Maybe we can push the house out."

Tom looks under the house. He looks at the tires. He lets some air out of one tire. The men let air out of all the tires.

Now there is half an inch[1] between the house and the bridge. The house is not stuck! The men get into their truck. They drive away with the house.

---

[1] 1.26 centimeters

3. PRONUNCIATION

Listen to your teacher. Say the words.

truck	men	is	we	Sam
stuck	get	it	he	have
under	let	in	three	half
of	says	inch	between	at
some		with		
what		bridge		

4. SPELLING

Listen to your teacher say the words. Write the missing letters. Then copy the words.

1. m_e_n   _____men_____

2. t___u___k   _____

3. pul___   _____

4. p___sh   _____

5. br___d___e   _____

6. ti___e   _____

5. VOCABULARY

What do you see in the pictures? Write the words.

pull the house   get out of the truck   let air out of the tire
push the house   get in the truck   drive under a bridge

1. _let air out of the tire_   2. _____   3. _____

4. _____   5. _____   6. _____

6. COMPREHENSION

Which sentence is correct? Circle a or b.

1. **a.** A man and a boy are in a truck.
   (b.) Three men are in a truck.

2. **a.** The truck is pulling a house.
   b. The truck is pushing a house.

3. **a.** The men drive under a bridge.
   b. The men drive over a hill.

4. **a.** The men are stuck under the bridge.
   b. The house is stuck under the bridge.

5. **a.** The men let air out of all the tires.
   b. The men let air out of some tires.

6. **a.** The men drive away with the house.
   b. The men drive away with the bridge.

7. WRITING

Write the sentences correctly.

1. Atruckispullingahouse.

   A truck is pulling a house.

2. Thehouseisstuckunderabridge.

   _____

3. Themenletairoutofallthetires.

   _____

4. Theydriveawaywiththehouse.

   _____

Binti to the Rescue

---

1. PRE-READING

- Look at the picture. What do you see?
- Say the words.
- Watch your teacher write the words.
- Copy the words onto the picture.

2. READING

- Listen to your teacher read the story. Look at the pictures.
- Listen to your teacher read the story again. Look at the words. Read the story.

Brian is three years old.
He is with his mother.
They are at the zoo.

They are going
to see the gorillas.

Brian runs to the gorillas.

He climbs a fence.

He falls.

He falls 18 feet.[1]

He is on the ground.
He doesn't move.

Brian is with the gorillas
now. Seven gorillas walk
to him.

One gorilla is a mother.
Her name is Binti. She
has her baby on her back.

[1] 5.5 meters

10

Binti picks up Brian.

11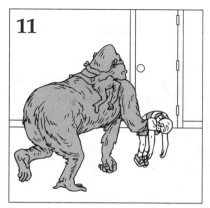

She carries him to a door.

12

She stands at the door.
She holds Brian.

13

She pats Brian
on the back.
Binti is a good mother!

14

A man comes to the door.
Binti gives Brian
to the man.

15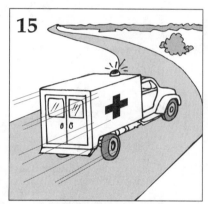

Brian goes to the hospital.

16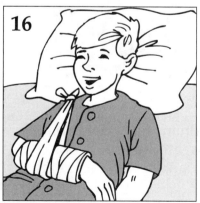

He has a broken arm, but
he is OK.

17

Brian's mother is happy.
"Thank you, Binti,"
she says.

- **Read the story again.**

Binti to the Rescue

Brian is three years old. He is with his mother. They are at the zoo.

They are going to see the gorillas. Brian runs to the gorillas. He climbs a fence.

He falls. He falls 18 feet.[1] He is on the ground. He doesn't move.

Brian is with the gorillas now. Seven gorillas walk to him. One gorilla is a mother. Her name is Binti. She has her baby on her back.

Binti picks up Brian. She carries him to a door. She stands at the door. She holds Brian. She pats Brian on the back. Binti is a good mother!

A man comes to the door. Binti gives Brian to the man.

Brian goes to the hospital. He has a broken arm, but he is OK.

Brian's mother is happy. "Thank you, Binti," she says.

---

[1] 5.5 meters

3. PRONUNCIATION

Listen to your teacher. Say the words.

go old hold broken	to move zoo you	mother come doesn't up but run	at pat back man stand happy	is his give pick with	he she see feet three

4. SPELLING

Listen to your teacher say the words. Write the missing letters. Then copy the words.

1. ye_a_rs _____*years*_____

2. m___the___ _____

3. c___im___ _____

4. ___en___e _____

5. m___ve _____

6. do___r _____

5. VOCABULARY

What do you see in the pictures? Write the words.

run   fall   carry
climb   pick up   pat

1. _*carry*_____   2. _____   3. _____

4. _____   5. _____   6. _____

6. COMPREHENSION

Circle YES or NO.

1. Brian is at the zoo with his mother.   (YES)   NO
2. They are going to see the penguins.   YES   NO
3. Brian runs to the gorillas.   YES   NO
4. He climbs a fence.   YES   NO
5. He falls.   YES   NO
6. He is with the gorillas.   YES   NO
7. One gorilla is Binti.   YES   NO
8. Binti is a father.   YES   NO
9. Binti pushes Brian with her nose.   YES   NO
10. Binti picks up Brian and carries him to a door.   YES   NO
11. She gives Brian to a man.   YES   NO
12. Brian has a broken arm, but he is OK.   YES   NO

7. WRITING

Copy your YES sentences.

Brian is at the zoo with his mother.

Where Is Mrs. Zimmer?

1. PRE-READING

- Look at the picture. What do you see?
- Say the words.
- Watch your teacher write the words.
- Copy the words onto the picture.

2. READING

- Listen to your teacher read the story. Look at the pictures.
- Listen to your teacher read the story again. Look at the words. Read the story.

1 Mr. and Mrs. Zimmer are in a van with their three children.

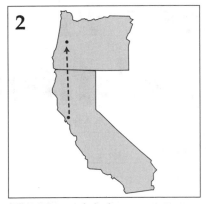

2 They are driving from California to Oregon.

3 It is late at night.

4 Mr. Zimmer is in the front seat. He is driving the van.

5 Mrs. Zimmer and the children are in the back seats. They are sleeping.

6 Mr. Zimmer is hungry. He stops at a fast-food restaurant.

7 He goes into the restaurant.

8 Mrs. Zimmer wakes up. She is hungry, too.

9 She goes into the restaurant.

Mrs. Zimmer walks
into the restaurant.
Mr. Zimmer walks
out of the restaurant.
Mr. Zimmer doesn't see
his wife.

Mr. Zimmer drives away
in the van.

He drives all night.

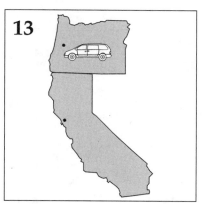

In the morning,
Mr. Zimmer and
the children are
in Oregon.

They get out of the van.

"Where's your mom?"
Mr. Zimmer asks
the children. "We don't
know," the children say.

Where is Mrs. Zimmer?

She is at the restaurant
in California!

• Read the story again.

Where Is Mrs. Zimmer?

Mr. and Mrs. Zimmer are in a van with their three children. They are driving from California to Oregon. It is late at night. Mr. Zimmer is in the front seat. He is driving the van. Mrs. Zimmer and the children are in the back seats. They are sleeping.

Mr. Zimmer is hungry. He stops at a fast-food restaurant. He goes into the restaurant. Mrs. Zimmer wakes up. She is hungry, too. She goes into the restaurant.

Mrs. Zimmer walks into the restaurant. Mr. Zimmer walks out of the restaurant. Mr. Zimmer doesn't see his wife.

Mr. Zimmer drives away in the van. He drives all night. In the morning, Mr. Zimmer and the children are in Oregon. They get out of the van. "Where's your mom?" Mr. Zimmer asks the children. "We don't know," the children say.

Where is Mrs. Zimmer? She is at the restaurant in California!

3. PRONUNCIATION

Listen to your teacher. Say the words.

late wake they	van at back fast ask	of from front up hungry doesn't	drive wife night	in it is his with	he see sleep seat

4. SPELLING

Listen to your teacher say the words. Write the missing letters. Then copy the words.

1. c _h_ ildr _e_ n   _children_
2. l___te   _____
3. ni___ ___t   _____
4. ___ung___y   _____
5. d___esn'___   _____
6. mo___nin___   _____
7. ___now   _____
8. w___er___   _____

5. VOCABULARY

What are the opposites? Write the words.

1. go   s _t_ _o_ _p_
2. day   n__ __ __t
3. go to sleep   __ __k__ u__
4. back   f__o__ __
5. get in   g__ __ o__ __

6. COMPREHENSION

Circle YES or NO.

1. Mr. and Mrs. Zimmer are in a van with their children.   (YES)   NO
2. Mr. Zimmer is driving the van.   YES   NO
3. The children are in the front seat.   YES   NO
4. They are going to Oregon.   YES   NO
5. It is late in the afternoon.   YES   NO
6. Mr. Zimmer stops at a restaurant.   YES   NO
7. He stops because he is tired.   YES   NO
8. Mrs. Zimmer goes into the restaurant, too.   YES   NO
9. Mr. Zimmer sees his wife in the restaurant.   YES   NO
10. Mr. Zimmer drives away.   YES   NO
11. In the morning, Mr. Zimmer is in Oregon.   YES   NO
12. Mrs. Zimmer is at the restaurant in California.   YES   NO

7. WRITING

Copy your YES sentences.

Mr. and Mrs. Zimmer are in a van with their children.

_____

_____

_____

_____

_____

_____

Fast Money

---

1. PRE-READING

- Look at the picture. What do you see?
- Say the words.
- Watch your teacher write the words.
- Copy the words onto the picture.

2. READING

- Listen to your teacher read the story. Look at the pictures.
- Listen to your teacher read the story again. Look at the words. Read the story.

1

MENU
HAMBURGER
FRIES   SM.   MED.   LG.
DRINKS   SM.   MED.   LG.

A man goes to a fast-food restaurant for lunch.

2

"Hi," a worker says. "May I help you?"

3

"I'd like a hamburger, large fries, and a medium Coke," the man says.

4

"Anything else?" the worker asks.

5

"No," the man answers. "That's it."

6

"Is that for here or to go?" the worker asks.

7

"To go," the man says.

8

The man pays for his lunch.

9

The worker puts the man's lunch in a bag.

10 The man takes the bag.

11 "Thank you," the worker says. "Have a nice day."

12 The man walks to a park.

13 He sits down and opens the bag. He is surprised.

14 There is no hamburger in the bag.
There are no french fries.
There is no Coke.

15 There is money in the bag—a lot of money!

16 The man counts the money. Two thousand dollars!

17 Why is the money in the bag?

18 The man doesn't know.
Do you know?
Can you guess?

(The answer is on page 89.)

• **Read the story again.**

Fast Money

A man goes to a fast-food restaurant for lunch. "Hi," a worker says. "May I help you?"

"I'd like a hamburger, large fries, and a medium Coke," the man says.

"Anything else?" the worker asks.

"No," the man answers. "That's it."

"Is that for here or to go?" the worker asks.

"To go," the man says.

The man pays for his lunch. The worker puts the man's lunch in a bag. The man takes the bag.

"Thank you," the worker says. "Have a nice day."

The man walks to a park. He sits down and opens the bag. He is surprised. There is no hamburger in the bag. There are no french fries. There is no Coke. There is money in the bag—a lot of money! The man counts the money. Two thousand dollars!

Why is the money in the bag? The man doesn't know. Do you know? Can you guess?

(The answer is on page 89.)

3. VOCABULARY

What do you see in the pictures? Write the words.

a park   large fries   a lot of money
an envelope   medium fries   a fast-food restaurant

1. <u>a fast-food restaurant</u> 2. _____ 3. _____

 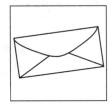 

4. _____ 5. _____ 6. _____

4. COMPREHENSION

Complete the sentences. Write the letter of your answer.

1. A man goes ___e___

2. He says, _____

3. A worker puts _____

4. The man takes the bag and walks _____

5. He opens the bag and finds _____

a. to a park.

b. a lot of money.

c. the man's lunch in a bag.

d. "I'd like a hamburger, large fries, and a medium Coke."

e. to a fast-food restaurant for lunch.

5. WRITING

Complete the sentences.

1. Where does the man go for lunch?

   He goes to a fast-food _restaurant_ .

2. What does the man want to eat?

   He wants a hamburger, large _____, and a _____ Coke.

3. Where does the worker put the man's lunch?

   She puts it in a _____ .

4. Where does the man go to eat his lunch?

   He goes to a _____ to eat his lunch.

5. What is in the bag?

   There is _____ in the bag—two _____ dollars.

6. Who put the money in the bag?

   The _____ of the restaurant put the money in the bag.

6. DISCUSSION

Ask your partner the questions. Circle your partner's answers.

1. Do you like hamburgers?   YES   NO
2. Do you like french fries?   YES   NO
3. Do you like Coke?   YES   NO
4. Do you like to eat at fast-food restaurants?   YES   NO
5. Do you like to eat at a park?   YES   NO

Returning a Favor

---

1. PRE-READING

- Look at the picture. What do you see?
- Say the words.
- Watch your teacher write the words.
- Copy the words onto the picture.

2. READING

- Listen to your teacher read the story. Look at the pictures.
- Listen to your teacher read the story again. Look at the words. Read the story.

1

It is 1965.

2

A little boy is at the beach with his parents.
He is four years old.

3

The boy is playing near the water.

4

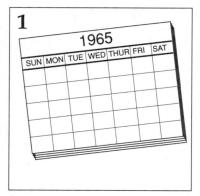

He walks into the water. His parents aren't watching him.

5

The water is over the boy's head!

6

A woman sees the boy. The woman's name is Mrs. Blaise.

7

Mrs. Blaise picks up the boy.

8

She carries him to his parents. "Thank you!" the boy's parents say.

9

It is 1975—ten years later.

10

The boy is
at the same beach.

11

He is 14 years old now.
He is big and strong.
He is a good swimmer.

12

A man is in the water.
The man can't swim.
"Help! Help!"
the man says.

13

The boy runs
into the water.

14

He swims to the man.

15

He pulls the man
to the beach.

16

"Thank you. Thank you,"
the man says.

17

Who is the man?

18

His name is Mr. Blaise.
He is Mrs. Blaise's
husband.

- **Read the story again.**

Returning a Favor

It is 1965. A little boy is at the beach with his parents. He is four years old.

The boy is playing near the water. He walks into the water. His parents aren't watching him.

The water is over the boy's head! A woman sees the boy. The woman's name is Mrs. Blaise. Mrs. Blaise picks up the boy. She carries him to his parents. "Thank you!" the boy's parents say.

It is 1975—ten years later. The boy is at the same beach. He is 14 years old now. He is big and strong. He is a good swimmer.

A man is in the water. The man can't swim. "Help! Help!" the man says.

The boy runs into the water. He swims to the man. He pulls the man to the beach. "Thank you. Thank you," the man says.

Who is the man? His name is Mr. Blaise. He is Mrs. Blaise's husband.

3. PRONUNCIATION

Listen to your teacher. Say the words.

he	play	is	water	to
see	say	his	walk	you
beach	name	him	strong	who
	same	swim		
	later	pick		
		with		

4. COMPREHENSION

When is it? Check (✓) your answer.

	1965	1975
1. The boy is four years old.	✓	
2. The boy is fourteen years old.		
3. The boy is at the beach with his parents.		
4. The boy is playing near the water.		
5. The boy is big and strong.		
6. A man is in the water. He can't swim.		
7. Mrs. Blaise picks up the boy and carries him to his parents.		
8. The boy runs into the water and swims to the man.		
9. "Thank you!" the boy's parents say.		
10. The boy pulls the man to the beach.		

5. VOCABULARY

What are the opposites? Write the words.

1. bad   g _o_ _o_ _d_

2. work   __ __ __ y

3. big   l __ __ t __ __

4. under   __ __ __ r

5. push   __ __ l __

6. different   s __ __ __

7. put down   __ __ c __ u __

6. WRITING

Complete the sentences.

A _____ _little_ _____ boy is playing at the beach. He walks into the
1

_____. The water is over the boy's _____!
2   3

A woman _____ up the boy and carries him to his
4

_____. The woman's _____ is
5   6

Mrs. Blaise.

Ten years later, the boy is at the _____ beach. A man is in
7

the water. He can't _____. " _____!" the
8   9

man says. The _____ swims to the man and pulls him to the
10

beach. The man's name is _____ Blaise. He is Mrs. Blaise's
11

_____.
12

Help! I Can't Find My Apartment!

1. PRE-READING

- Look at the picture. What do you see?
- Say the words.
- Watch your teacher write the words.
- Copy the words onto the picture.

2. READING

- Listen to your teacher read the story. Look at the pictures.
- Listen to your teacher read the story again. Look at the words. Read the story.

1

Erik lives in Norway.

2

He lives in the country.
He doesn't like the country.

3

He wants to live
in the city.

4

Erik goes to Oslo.
Oslo is a big city.

5

He finds a nice apartment.

6

He pays some money
for the apartment.

7

Erik is hungry.
He goes to a restaurant.
He eats lunch.

8

After lunch,
Erik wants to go back
to his new apartment.

9

Where is his apartment
building?
He can't remember!

10 "My apartment building is big," Erik thinks. He looks for a big apartment building.

11 Many apartment buildings are big!

12 "My apartment building is gray," Erik thinks. He looks for a gray apartment building.

13 Many apartment buildings are gray!

14 "My apartment building is on a busy street," Erik thinks. He looks for an apartment building on a busy street.

15 Many apartment buildings are on busy streets!

16 Erik looks for his apartment building for one month. He can't find it!

- **Read the story again.**

Help! I Can't Find My Apartment!

Erik lives in Norway. He lives in the country. He doesn't like the country. He wants to live in the city.

Erik goes to Oslo. Oslo is a big city. He finds a nice apartment. He pays some money for the apartment.

Erik is hungry. He goes to a restaurant. He eats lunch.

After lunch, Erik wants to go back to his new apartment. Where is his apartment building? He can't remember!

"My apartment building is big," Erik thinks. He looks for a big apartment building. Many apartment buildings are big!

"My apartment building is gray," Erik thinks. He looks for a gray apartment building. Many apartment buildings are gray!

"My apartment building is on a busy street," Erik thinks. He looks for an apartment building on a busy street. Many apartment buildings are on busy streets!

Erik looks for his apartment building for one month. He can't find it!

3. PRONUNCIATION

Listen to your teacher. Say the words.

in	lunch
is	hungry
his	month
live	some
city	money
building	country
busy	

4. SPELLING

Listen to your teacher say the words. Write the missing letters. Then copy the words.

1. w _a_ nt   _want_

2. ___ity   _____

3. fin___   _____

4. ni___e   _____

5. ap___rtme___t   _____

6. m___n___y   _____

7. ___u___ch   _____

8. bus___   _____

5. VOCABULARY

What do you see in the pictures? Write the words.

the country
a big city

a nice apartment
Norway

an apartment building
a busy street

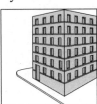

1. _a big city_ _____

2. _____

3. _____

4. _____

5. _____

6. _____

6. COMPREHENSION

Which sentence is correct? Circle a or b.

1. **a.** Erik wants to live in the country.
   (b.) Erik wants to live in the city.

2. **a.** He goes to Oslo and finds a nice apartment.
   b. He goes to Oslo and finds a nice street.

3. **a.** He eats lunch at his apartment.
   b. He eats lunch at a restaurant.

4. **a.** After lunch he wants to go back to the country.
   b. After lunch he wants to go back to his apartment.

5. **a.** He can't find his apartment building.
   b. He can find his apartment building.

7. WRITING

Complete the sentences.

1. Erik finds a nice apartment in the city.

   Erik finds __a__ nice __apartment__ in the ___city___ .

   Erik _____ ____ nice _____ in ____ _____ .

   _____ _____ ____ _____ _____ ___ ____ _____ .

2. He eats lunch at a restaurant.

   He eats _____ at a _____ .

   _____ eats _____ _____ a _____ .

   ____ _____ _____ ____ __ _____ .

3. He can't find his apartment building.

   He can't _____ his apartment _____ .

   He _____ _____ his _____ _____ .

   _____ _____ _____ _____ _____ _____ .

A Big Tip

---

1. PRE-READING

- Look at the picture. What do you see?
- Say the words.
- Watch your teacher write the words.
- Copy the words onto the picture.

2. READING

- Listen to your teacher read the story. Look at the pictures.
- Listen to your teacher read the story again. Look at the words. Read the story.

1

Bob likes to eat spaghetti.

2

Every Friday he goes to an Italian restaurant and eats spaghetti for lunch.

3

Phyllis is a waitress at the Italian restaurant.

4

Phyllis and Bob always talk and laugh.
They are good friends.

5

After Bob eats, he pays for his lunch.

6

Then he puts some money on the table. The money is for Phyllis. It is her tip.

7

One day Bob eats spaghetti at the restaurant.

8

He pays for his lunch.

9

Then he asks Phyllis, "Do you want a tip today? Or do you want half of my lottery ticket?'

10

"Half of your lottery
ticket?" Phyllis asks.

11

"Yes," Bob says.
"I have a lottery ticket.
If I win the lottery,
you get half of the money."

12

Phyllis laughs.
"OK," she says. "I don't
want a tip today.
I want half
of the lottery money!"
She laughs again.

13

The next day, Bob wins
the lottery.
He wins six million dollars.

14

Bob goes to the Italian
restaurant.

15

"Here is your tip,"
Bob tells Phyllis.
"Three million dollars!"

• Read the story again.

A Big Tip

Bob likes to eat spaghetti. Every Friday he goes to an Italian restaurant and eats spaghetti for lunch.

Phyllis is a waitress at the Italian restaurant. Phyllis and Bob always talk and laugh. They are good friends.

After Bob eats, he pays for his lunch. Then he puts some money on the table. The money is for Phyllis. It is her tip.

One day Bob eats spaghetti at the restaurant. He pays for his lunch. Then he asks Phyllis, "Do you want a tip today? Or do you want half of my lottery ticket?"

"Half of your lottery ticket?" Phyllis asks.

"Yes," Bob says. "I have a lottery ticket. If I win the lottery, you get half of the money."

Phyllis laughs. "OK," she says. "I don't want a tip today. I want half of the lottery money!" She laughs again.

The next day, Bob wins the lottery. He wins six million dollars.

Bob goes to the Italian restaurant. "Here is your tip," Bob tells Phyllis. "Three million dollars!"

3. PRONUNCIATION

Listen to your teacher. Say the words.

laugh	then	Bob	lunch	tip
half	again	want	money	ticket
after	every	lottery	some	give
have	next	dollar	what	win
ask	says		of	six
				Phyllis

4. SPELLING

Listen to your teacher say the words. Write the missing letters. Then copy the words.

1. Fr_i_da_y_ _____Friday_____

2. l___n___h _____

3. fr___en___ _____

4. m___n___y _____

5. ___abl___ _____

6. pa___ _____

7. ha___f _____

8. ti___k___t _____

5. VOCABULARY

What do you see in the pictures? Write the words.

spaghetti	lottery ticket	waitress
restaurant	half of a lottery ticket	tip

1. _restaurant_   2. _____   3. _____

4. _____   5. _____   6. _____

6. COMPREHENSION

Complete the sentences. Write the letter of your answer.

1. Bob likes to eat __*e*__

2. Every Friday he goes _____

3. Phyllis is _____

4. Bob asks Phyllis, _____

5. Bob wins _____

6. He gives Phyllis _____

a. a waitress.

b. half of the money—
three million dollars!

c. "Do you want a tip today? Or do
you want half of my lottery ticket?"

d. the lottery.

e. spaghetti.

f. to an Italian restaurant.

7. WRITING

Answer the questions. Complete the sentences.

1. What does Bob like to eat?

   He likes to eat __*spaghetti*__.

2. Where does Bob go every Friday?

   He goes to an _____ restaurant.

3. Who is Phyllis?

   She is a _____ at the restaurant.

4. What does Bob ask Phyllis?

   He asks her, "Do you want a _____ today? Or do you want half of

   my lottery ticket?"

5. What does Phyllis say?

   She says, "I want _____ of the lottery money!"

6. How much money does Bob win?

   He wins _____ million dollars.

7. How much money does Bob give Phyllis?

   He gives her three _____ dollars.

The original newspaper and magazine versions of *Very Easy True Stories* contain information that could not be included in the adaptations. Sometimes the information was too complicated to include; sometimes including it would have made the stories too long for the allotted space. On the other hand, the information—in many cases, the story behind the story—was just too interesting to leave out entirely. So, it was decided that additional facts would be given here, in a special "To the Teacher" section.

As you will see from the sophistication of the language, this section is not meant to be read by students. If, however, you think the information adds interest or clarity to a story, you could share it with students.

Unit 1

SHOPPING DAY

Rara's owners often took their pet penguin on the quarter-mile walk to the local fish market. When Rara began disappearing occasionally, his owners discovered that Rara was going to the market on his own.

The owner of the fish shop keeps track of Rara's purchases and sends a bill to his owners. She says that Rara eats only the freshest fish. Mackerel and sardines are his favorites.

Unit 2

MARY WALKS HOME

Mary works 44 hours a week in a bank in downtown Philadelphia. Her job is sorting out the accounts of recently deceased people. The job is stressful, Mary told the Associated Press, and the eight-mile walk home helps her leave her worries at work.

Mary's last name, by the way, is Walker.

Unit 3

ELEVATOR ROMANCE

The stuck elevator was in Karlstad, Sweden.

None of the Swedish newspapers took a photo of the couple, so an authentic photo was not available.

The photo that accompanies the story was supplied by a Swedish photo agency and is of an anonymous Swedish couple.

Unit 4

A SON FOR MR. AND MRS. AVERSA?

Mrs. Aversa was not taking fertility drugs. The odds against all four babies being girls were three million to one.

The Aversas do not plan on having more children. Mr. Aversa, who is Italian, hopes at least one of his six daughters will share his passion for watching soccer games on TV.

Unit 5

IS THERE A FACE ON MARS?

The photo that revealed the famous face on Mars was taken from the *U.S. Viking I* orbiter from a distance of 1,873 kilometers (1,162 miles). The face is one and a half times longer than San Francisco's Golden Gate Bridge and as tall as New York's World Trade Center.

The *Mars Pathfinder* land rover, which landed on Mars in 1997, did not photograph the Cydonia region where the face is located; this disappointed those who believe that the face is a calling card left by alien visitors to our solar system long ago.

Unit 6

NEIGHBORS

Jack's real name is Jake, and Ann's real name is Blanche. Students who participated in field testing *Very Easy True Stories* had difficulty recognizing "Jake" and "Blanche" as people's names, so the names were changed.

Jake and Blanche's arrangement was first reported by Naomi Dunavan in the *Grand Forks Herald*, in an article titled "A His and Hers Marriage." The story was picked up by the wire services, and before long reporters and television crews from all over the country were beating a path to Blanche and Jake's door . . . that is, doors.

Why didn't Jake and Blanche divorce? Blanche told the *Grand Forks Herald* that she didn't believe in it. "There was no reason to get a divorce," she said. "We had our good years, we had a good marriage to start with, and we took trips with the kids. We always worked together and did projects together. But, as far as living together, that was a horse of a different color." Jake agreed that divorce was never an option. "We're too old, and it costs too much," he said. When asked if they suggested this arrangement for other married couples, Blanche replied, "Well, it sure works for us."

Unit 7

A SMART MOTHER

Tasha is a Belgian Malinois. Tasha's owner told the *San Diego Union Tribune* that the look in Tasha's eyes as she pushed her puppies in her food dish was not one of fear. "It was something like 'Big dummy, what are you doing leaving me alone?'" Now, whenever Tasha hears raindrops hit the roof, she picks up her puppies and puts them up on the furniture. Then she climbs up with them. She and the puppies won't come down until the rain stops.

Unit 8

STUCK!

Traffic came to a complete halt on U.S. Highway 17 in Wilmington, North Carolina, when a cottage being moved got stuck under an overpass. For 45 minutes, the movers discussed their options and then came up with a simple solution: They let some air out of the truck's tires.

Unit 9

BINTI TO THE RESCUE

Born at the Columbus Zoo, Binti was taken from her mother at two months because her mother didn't have enough milk. She was raised by humans who worked in three shifts so that she could be held constantly, as her mother would have held her. When she was six, she became pregnant. Worried that she had no maternal role model, trainers gave Binti mothering lessons, using a stuffed doll to teach her to care for her baby. When her baby was born, Binti turned out to be a "great mom—better than we expected," in the words of one of her trainers.

When Binti went to the rescue of Brian, with her own baby on her back, some people attributed her gentleness to her extensive experience with humans. Animal behaviorists, however, suggested that Binti would probably have come to Brian's rescue even if she hadn't been raised and trained by humans. One expert on primates told *USA Today* that he found it "not surprising that a lactating female would pick up an injured infant from a related species."

Surprising or not, Binti's response to Brian's fall at Chicago's Brookfield Zoo attracted attention from as far away as Ireland and Argentina. It prompted many people to send Binti gifts, including one 25-pound gift of bananas.

Unit 10

WHERE IS MRS. ZIMMER?

After a vacation in San Francisco, Mr. and Mrs. Zimmer and their three children piled into their van for the all-night trip home to Eugene, Oregon. It was somewhere along Interstate 5 that Mrs. Zimmer got stranded at a fast-food restaurant. "I never saw him leave," Mrs. Zimmer told the Associated Press. "I guess he didn't see me, either. I sat down and ate my burger. I looked out the window just in time to see my van going up the ramp onto I-5 with my husband and my children in it. Needless to say, I was shocked."

Mrs. Zimmer waited at the restaurant for three hours, and then she took a bus home to Oregon. She arrived in Eugene at noon the next day and was reunited with her frantic husband. He told police he thought he had left his wife in Redding, California, but Redding police found no trace of her. Actually she was stranded in Red Bluff, thirty miles south of Redding.

Unit 11

FAST MONEY

The fast-food restaurant was a Taco Bell near Detroit, Michigan; it was actually chicken tacos, not a hamburger and fries, that the man ordered. His order was changed to a hamburger and fries in the *True Stories* version of the story to make the vocabulary more accessible.

The man returned to the restaurant with the cash ($2,480, to be exact) immediately. The restaurant manager, who thought he'd never see the money again, gave him a big hug. Taco Bell rewarded the man with a certificate good for six months of free food at the restaurant.

Unit 12

RETURNING A FAVOR

Mr. Blaise, who could not swim, lost his balance and fell from a cabin cruiser that was moored about 250 feet from a beach in Salem, Massachusetts. The boy, Roger Lausier, heard Mrs. Blaise screaming for help and rescued her husband. Roger was commended by the Massachusetts Humane Society for his bravery and honored in a ceremony. It was not until the ceremony that the two families began to talk and realized that Mrs. Blaise was the woman who had rescued Roger in 1965.

Unit 13

HELP! I CAN'T FIND MY APARTMENT!

The man who couldn't find his apartment was actually named Jermund. Students, as well as teachers, who participated in field-testing *Very Easy True Stories* were uncertain how to pronounce "Jermund," so the name was changed to "Erik."

When Jermund went to a cafe for lunch, he forgot to take his new address with him.

After looking for his apartment building for a month without success, Jermund went to the offices of the *Aftenposten* newspaper and explained his predica-ment. The newspaper ran Jermund's story and a photo of him in the hope that Jermund's landlady would recognize him and contact him. Reporters at the *Aftenposten* never heard from Jermund again. They assume that the landlady contacted Jermund and that he found his apartment, but they don't know for sure.

Jermund paid one month's rent for the thirty minutes he spent in his apartment.

Unit 14

A BIG TIP

Robert Cunningham, a fifty-five-year-old police officer, frequented Sal's Pizzeria, where he ate linguine with clam sauce and joked with Phyllis Penzo, who had been a waitress at Sal's for twenty-four years. "We were kidding around," Cunningham told the *New York Times*, "and I told her if I won it would be her tip. But she knows my word is as good as gold."

The six-million-dollar prize is being paid in twenty yearly installments. Cunningham and Penzo each receive $142,800 a year.

Answer Key

UNIT 1

4. Spelling
1. family 2. Monday 3. back 4. walk 5. look 6. take
7. home 8. thank

5. Vocabulary
1. fish market 2. every Monday 3. penguin 4. a family in Japan 5. 12 small fish 6. backpack

6. Comprehension
1. a 2. b 3. a 4. b 5. b 6. a

7. Writing
1. Rara is a penguin. 2. Every Monday Rara goes shopping.
3. He walks to the fish market. 4. He eats 12 fish at the market.
5. He takes some fish for his family. 6. He walks home with the fish.

UNIT 2

3. Vocabulary
1. go to bed 2. drive 3. eat dinner 4. walk 5. take the bus
6. take the train

4. Comprehension
1. b 2. b 3. b 4. a 5. a 6. b

UNIT 3

3. Spelling
1. talk 2. walk 3. tired 4. hungry 5. thirsty 6. month
7. later 8. married

4. Vocabulary
1. a hungry woman 2. an elevator 3. two people in love
4. a tired woman 5. a thirsty man

5. Comprehension
1. b 2. b 3. b 4. a 5. b

6. Writing
1. woman 2. stuck 3. elevator 4. open 5. thirsty 6. love

UNIT 4

4. Spelling
1. love 2. very 3. much 4. doctor 5. babies 6. another
7. daughter 8. son

5. Vocabulary
1. the first baby 2. the second baby 3. the third baby
4. the fourth baby

6. Comprehension
1. c 2. e 3. b 4. a 5. d

7. Writing
1. expecting 2. two 3. doctor 4. four 5. girl 6. baby
7. fourth 8. more

UNIT 5

4. Spelling
1. take 2. face 3. newspaper 4. people 5. wide 6. hill
7. light 8. think

5. Vocabulary
1. hill 2. spaceship 3. face 4. shadow 5. newspaper
6. scientist

6. Comprehension
1. c 2. e 3. a 4. d 5. b

7. Writing
1. Mars 2. camera 3. takes 4. face 5. mile 6. shadow

UNIT 6

4. Vocabulary
1. smoke 2. watch baseball on TV 3. listen to music 4. snore
5. move in

5. Comprehension
1. b 2. e 3. d 4. a 5. c

6. Writing
1. Jack and Ann are married, but they are not happy. 2. They are very different. 3. Ann buys the house next door. 4. She moves in. 5. Now Ann is Jack's neighbor.

UNIT 7

3. Vocabulary
1. California 2. puppies 3. clothes 4. bowl 5. yard
6. books

4. Comprehension
1. YES 2. YES 3. NO 4. YES 5. YES 6. NO 7. NO
8. YES 9. YES 10. YES 11. YES

UNIT 8

4. Spelling
1. men 2. truck 3. pull 4. push 5. bridge 6. tire

5. Vocabulary
1. let air out of the tire 2. get in the truck 3. push the house
4. drive under a bridge 5. pull the house 6. get out of the truck

6. Comprehension
1. b 2. a 3. a 4. b 5. a 6. a

7. Writing
1. A truck is pulling a house. 2. The house is stuck under a bridge. 3. The men let air out of all the tires. 4. They drive away with the house.

UNIT 9

4. Spelling
1. years **2.** mother **3.** climb **4.** fence **5.** move **6.** door

5. Vocabulary
1. carry **2.** pat **3.** fall **4.** run **5.** pick up **6.** climb

6. Comprehension
1. YES **2.** NO **3.** YES **4.** YES **5.** YES **6.** YES **7.** YES
8. NO **9.** NO **10.** YES **11.** YES **12.** YES

UNIT 10

4. Spelling
1. children **2.** late **3.** night **4.** hungry **5.** doesn't
6. morning **7.** know **8.** where

5. Vocabulary
1. stop **2.** night **3.** wake up **4.** front **5.** get out

6. Comprehension
1. YES **2.** YES **3.** NO **4.** YES **5.** NO **6.** YES **7.** NO
8. YES **9.** NO **10.** YES **11.** YES **12.** YES

UNIT 11

3. Vocabulary
1. a fast-food restaurant **2.** a lot of money **3.** medium fries
4. large fries **5.** an envelope **6.** a park

4. Comprehension
1. e **2.** d **3.** c **4.** a **5.** b

5. Writing
1. restaurant **2.** fries, medium **3.** bag **4.** park **5.** money,
thousand **6.** manager

1

The manager of the
fast-food restaurant
needs to go to the
bank.

2

He puts two
thousand dollars
in an envelope.

3

He puts
the envelope
in a bag.

4

He puts the bag
down.

5

The man takes
the bag.

6

Now the man has two
thousand dollars,

7

and the manager
has a hamburger,
fries, and a Coke!

UNIT 12

4. Comprehension
1. 1965 **2.** 1975 **3.** 1965 **4.** 1965 **5.** 1975 **6.** 1975
7. 1965 **8.** 1975 **9.** 1965 **10.** 1975

5. Vocabulary
1. good **2.** play **3.** little **4.** over **5.** pull **6.** same
7. pick up

6. Writing
1. little **2.** water **3.** head **4.** picks **5.** parents **6.** name
7. same **8.** swim **9.** Help **10.** boy **11.** Mr. **12.** husband

UNIT 13

4. Spelling
1. want **2.** city **3.** find **4.** nice **5.** apartment **6.** money
7. lunch **8.** busy

5. Vocabulary
1. a big city **2.** a busy street **3.** an apartment building
4. a nice apartment **5.** the country **6.** Norway

6. Comprehension
1. b **2.** a **3.** b **4.** b **5.** a

UNIT 14

4. Spelling
1. Friday **2.** lunch **3.** friend **4.** money **5.** table **6.** pay
7. half **8.** ticket

5. Vocabulary
1. restaurant **2.** waitress **3.** tip **4.** spaghetti **5.** lottery ticket
6. half of a lottery ticket

6. Comprehension
1. e **2.** f **3.** a **4.** c **5.** d **6.** b

7. Writing
1. spaghetti **2.** Italian **3.** waitress **4.** tip **5.** half **6.** six
7. million

ACKNOWLEDGMENTS

I wish to thank:

• Sharron Bassano, who read an early version of the manuscript and whose suggestions were, as always, exactly right;

• Jorge Islas, an extraordinary teacher, who helped me field-test the stories in his class of adult learners;

• Kathleen Mitchell, ESL teacher at Whitewater (Wisconsin) Middle School, who opened her classroom to me so that I could expand my field testing to younger students;

• Joan Morley, Linguistics Professor at the University of Michigan, who took some time at a busy TESOL conference to give me some advice about the pronunciation exercise;

• Hirokiyo Nomura at the *Kumamoto Nichi-Nichi Shimbun*, who verified the story "Shopping Day";

• Toshie Noji, who translated materials for "Shopping Day";

• Waterford, Michigan, police officer Nick Petranovic, who verified the story "Fast Money";

• Barbara Driscoll at the Massachusetts Humane Society, who verified the story "Returning a Favor";

• the many reference librarians and newspaper reporters who provided photos, clippings, and leads;

• Robert Ruvo, associate production editor, who skillfully guided this book through its final stages;

• the people at Addison Wesley Longman—Joanne Dresner, Laura McCormick, Allen Ascher, and Halley Gatenby—and my editor, Penny Laporte, who continue to share my enthusiasm for all the *True Stories*.

PHOTO CREDITS

We wish to thank the following for providing us with photographs.

Unit 1
Shopping Day
Stan Grossfeld / *The Boston Globe*

Unit 2
Mary Walks Home
Wide World Photos

Unit 3
Elevator Romance
Tiofoto

Unit 4
A Son for Mr. and Mrs. Aversa?
South West News Service

Unit 5
Is There a Face on Mars?
Courtesy of NASA

Unit 6
Neighbors
Courtesy of the *Grand Forks Herald*

Unit 7
A Smart Mother
Scott Lionnett / *San Diego Union Tribune*
page 42, *Weekly World News* (photos of dog, bird, rabbit, and cat)
page 42, Robert Pickett / Corbis (photo of goldfish)
page 42, Riad Twal (photo of hamster)

Unit 8
Stuck!
UPI / Corbis-Bettmann

Unit 9
Binti to the Rescue
Copyright 1997, *USA Today*. Reprinted with permission.

Unit 10
Where Is Mrs. Zimmer?
© TSM / Jon Feingersh, 1997

Unit 11
Fast Money
Sandra Heyer

Unit 12
Returning a Favor
Kelly-Mooney Photography / Corbis

Unit 13
Help! I Can't Find My Apartment!
Karina Jensen / Scanfoto

Unit 14
A Big Tip
Mark Vergari / Gannett Newspapers